Coming Straight From My Heart
Vol. I

Jamie Lynn Cusick
(Dictated to Cheryl Cusick)

DENVER, COLORADO

The opinions expressed in this manuscript are solely the opinions of the author and do not represent the opinions or thoughts of the publisher. The author has represented and warranted full ownership and/or legal right to publish all the materials in this book.

Coming Straight From My Heart Vol. I
All Rights Reserved.
Copyright © 2015 Jamie Lynn Cusick (Dictated to Cheryl Cusick)
v1.0

This book may not be reproduced, transmitted, or stored in whole or in part by any means, including graphic, electronic, or mechanical without the express written consent of the publisher except in the case of brief quotations embodied in critical articles and reviews.

Outskirts Press, Inc.
http://www.outskirtspress.com

ISBN: 978-1-4327-5770-0

Outskirts Press and the "OP" logo are trademarks belonging to Outskirts Press, Inc.

PRINTED IN THE UNITED STATES OF AMERICA

Contents

Thinking of You	1
You Are Special	2
Dreams Make Us Unique	3
Entity	4
I Am	5
The Best Is Yet to Come	6
Love Don't Need a Reason	7
Wanting	8
Will You?	9
You've Always	10
Comfort	11
Same Place	12
Alone	13
Time Flies	14
Glowing	15
Portrait of My Heart	16
Question	17
You Don't Understand	18
Friendship	19
The Blame	20
Thank You	21
True Friendship	22
Chad	23
Shelly	24
MDA Summer Camp	25
Never Again	26
Cherish the Thoughts	27
You Are Always Here	28

I Need You	29
The Way I Feel	30
The Hands of Time Move Forward	31
My Cries	32
The Skies Grow Darker	33
My Heart and Soul Cry Out	34
The Masterpiece	35
Separation	36
Suffering	37
The Remains of My Broken Heart	38
Shattered Dreams	40
Tranquility	41
The Light of My Heart	42
Tremble	43

Thinking of You

I am sitting in front of the TV
Although my body is here
My mind is not
I am thinking of someone
Whom I've been thinking of a lot
I'm thinking of what you might be doing
If you are thinking of me too
I'm thinking of how you are
If you are as lonely as I am
I'd love to have at least
One day to spend with you
I miss you and am thinking of you

You Are Special

I've been walking down the street
The one I used to call my own
I can't say that now
It belongs to everyone

I used to keep to myself
Now I guess I still do
But something in me changed
Since the day I met you

Behind your eyes are a lot of secrets
Different topics to discuss
If you ever want or need to talk
I'm always available

You're one of those people
You very seldom meet
You're a friend to those who need one
YOU ARE SPECIAL!

Dreams Make Us Unique

You have to live your dreams
Don't let people stop you, put you down
They're going to try and take it all
Don't let them
It's yours

You have to hold on to your dreams
Dreams will pass you by
Don't let them
It's yours

You have to believe in your dreams
Dreams are what make us carry on
They make us unique!

Entity

I hope you know
How deeply you've touched me
When I'm having a bad day
All I have to do is look at you
Just to say "hi"
You make me feel good
Just to know someone cares
There are not, nor will there ever be,
Enough words for me to express to you
My gratitude, nor are there enough words
To express my thanks for your kindness
There is not a day goes by
That you aren't thought of by me
I hope that as the years pass
You remember me
For you are always in my heart
I'll remember and love you
Always and forever

I Am

I see your every move
I feel your every emotion
I know your every need
I am the air you breathe
I am the dream in your sleep
I am the warmth in your heart
I am the one to trust
I am the one to love
I am the friend you need
That you thought never existed
Open your eyes!!!
I will always be by your side
I will always be here for you

The Best Is Yet to Come

As the years pass and beat against
this cold and weary heart
I will hold my head high
For I know the best is yet to come

No one will force me to give up, back up, or shut up
For I know the best is yet to come

And when the world deals me its worst
And I walk alone
I shall hold my head high, standing straight,
and walk proud
For I know the best is yet to come

Love Don't Need a Reason

Just a little more time is all we need
Just a little more
For all to believe
Just for all to join hands
And all to help each other
Cause love don't need a reason
Cause love don't have limits
We can all stand tall together
Cause love don't need a reason

Wanting

My soul burns with passion
Every time I see your face
My heart's desire of wanting you here with me
As a part of my life
I'll spoil you with the riches of the purest gold
I'll climb the highest mountain
I'll dive the deepest ocean
Forge the dark and fear
Because I want you here
The sight of you sets me free
You are the creature that captured my heart and soul

Will You?

Will you be my friend?
Will you talk with me?
Will you spend time with me?
Will you listen to me?
Will you understand me?
Will you trust me?
Will you laugh with me?
Will you cry with me?
Will you be there for me?

You've Always

You've brightened my life in so many ways
You've touched the very soul of me
You've opened my eyes to a different light
You've helped me with so much
You've always been there
You've always made time
You've always listened
You've always cared
You've wiped tears from my eyes
You've helped me spread my wings and fly

Comfort

I think of you often
Just to let you know
How deep for you my love is
And the rate at which it grows
I know you love me
From you I'll never stray
Whenever I'm in trouble
You'll come my way
I'm glad you're a part of my life
I love you so very much
On someone I can always
Depend, count and trust

Same Place

Why can't I say the things I need to say?
Every time I try, the words just get in the way

I want to tell you the way I feel
Something like this has to be real

The feeling I get when I see your face
Just to know we're in the same place

Will I ever find the courage deep in my soul?
To tell you, "I love you" and the way it grows?

Alone

All alone
I scream
No one hears
The walls
The walls are closing in
The rain
Wet and cold
Beating against my body
Shaking
Screaming
Shivering
No one hears
All alone the walls close in

Time Flies

I know just how to win and I know just how to lose
I know just when to dream and
I know when to face the truth
I know time is definitely going to fly
I know I'll never tell you all the things I've got to tell you
But I know I had to give it a try
I know how it is and I know how I want it to be
I know how much I love you and I know I've got to make you see

Glowing

Just to see you
Just to hear mention of your name
It sets me free
You are the sun in my sky
You always shine
Your eyes are the stars in my Heaven
Which are always twinkling
Always bringing a smile
Your soul is a burning candle
Always glowing
Your spirit is a breath of fresh air
That lifts my spirits

Portrait of My Heart

Look what I've done
I've torn it apart
The beautiful portrait of our friendship
Which was just starting to bloom
And now it may never continue to grow
No one is to blame but myself
The thoughtless & careless words that I've said
I've sunk so low
Now I'm empty again inside
Nothing left but memories
And I take hold of them
Grasp them so tight it hurts
Re-living each minute
Minute by precious minute
And I wonder
Can it be salvaged?

Question

Whatever happened to the
love that we once knew

Whatever happened to the
trust that we once shared

Whatever happened to the
friend I thought I found in you

Whatever happened to the
times when the sky was blue

Whatever happened to me?
The selflessness shared between two

You Don't Understand

You don't get it
Why is it that you won't understand?
What can I do?
Is there nothing I can say?
I am the helping hand you feel
I am the one who's here for you
Just turn around and you'll see
That the life-saving friend
Is me

Friendship

Once in a while
You find someone
To talk, laugh, and share things with
And to place your trust within
People like you are hard to find
You're very special, one of a kind
The love expressed between two friends
Like you and I, it has no end
Our friendship is like that of a rose
It has bloomed and now continues to grow

The Blame

The fear that dwells within me
is much more than I can bear
My mind draws a blank
as to the reason that it's there
It's just not the same now
nor will it ever be
And the blame is placed upon its rightful owner
in this situation, it's me

Thank You

Today isn't a special day
I just wanted to send a smile your way

For being whom you are - so nice and so caring
Thank you for loving, thank you for sharing

People like you are very hard to find
Someone to love, respect, and admire all of the time

Just to say thank you for all that you do
Making people feel wonderful - just by being you

True Friendship

If there's one thing that I'm sure of
In this world that changes from day to day
It's the friend that I have in you
A friendship that continues to grow and will never sway

A place full of cold, unfriendly faces
True friends are very hard to find
But God sent you my way
A friendship to stand the test of time

When the obstacles of life stand in my way
You're always there and you genuinely care
With words of love and words of encouragement
Thank you for all that you share

I will always be grateful for the bond that we have
And I'll always be thankful for all that you do
There's just one more thing that I have to say
My dear and special friend - I LOVE YOU!

Chad

I never got the chance to meet you face to face
Before the day came that you had to go away

But I've always seen you in my heart
And were my inspiration each and every day

The challenges life had in store for you
You faced them all with a smile

Such grace and courage
Such dignity and style

We love you and miss you, my dear friend
The pain you suffered has come to an end

Not a day goes by that you aren't thought of
We feel your love returned from above

Shelly

It's been over a year my friend
But the pain is still immense, will it ever end?
I still sleep with my blinds up at night
It brings me closer to you, as you silence my fright
You're always beside me and in my heart
You and I will never part

There's nothing in this world that I can't do now
For you're living in me, it gives me the strength somehow
To carry on without you here
Is very hard but I have no fear
You pick me up whenever I fall
And you're always there when I call

I feel you hold me close when I'm in doubt
You're what friendship is all about
My love for you will never die
I feel you return it all the way from the sky

MDA Summer Camp

Just to say thank you for being part of my life
For always being there, through celebration and strife
The friendships that come in laughter and tears
Helped me grow into a strong individual
through the years

Just to say thank you for the love you share
Your compassion has been shown, your trust,
and your care
The memories I will hold close to my heart,
The ups and the downs, from now back to the start

Just to say thank you for giving a special meaning to life,
A hug, a smile, a talk in the night
You've pick me up to soar on the wings of a dove,
For the rest of my life, I will testify to love

Never Again

Why does this always happen?Is there no end?
Everything gets destroyed and I feel alone
Not knowing why or how this happens
But somehow knowing that I am to blame

Don't try to look at it, I won't show it to you
It seems that this has happened again and there is no cure
No remedy for that way I feel inside
Sunk so low, so empty, so scared

No more mistakes will I make, ever again
I promise it won't see the light of day
No one seems to care about it, no one understands
No one and nothing, that's all I have

Cherish the Thoughts

The skies are growing dark all around me
The rainbow that once shined so bright is now gone
And there is no chance for its return

How I want it to come back to me
The way the colors would dance among the clouds
But I know that it never will

It always brought sunshine to me
Even on the darkest days when there was no end in sight
My one true friend, my constant companion

I feel so lost and so alone without the rainbow
No one seems to understand or take the time to care
A lasting memory is all I have left

I will always cherish the thoughts
Hold them dear to my heart
Forever remembering

You Are Always Here

Whatever comes my way
Whatever is thrown in my face
I know you are always there
To comfort me with your warm embrace

When nothing goes my way
When everything falls apart
I trust that you'll always be there
You've been beside me from the start

Whenever I feel like giving up
When I feel I can't go on
I hear your words of encouragement
As you help me through the storm

You are the reason I live
You are the reason I breathe
You give me what I long for
The joy and the comfort and the peace

I Need You

Counting the hours that I sit alone
I am waiting for your smiling face
The way you used to calm my soul
Just by speaking one word

I need you here with me, to love me
To tell me that everything's going to be all right
It won't happen and it never will
I don't understand why it can't

I played the game but there was no prize at the end
I just want to share everything with you
Just dreaming of having the chance to let you know
Can't you see it is supposed to be?

The Way I Feel

It wasn't supposed to happen to me
I wasn't planning on something like this
I would keep the feelings locked up inside
Never to see the light of day

All of that has been erased because of you
What I wouldn't do for the chance
To tell you exactly how I feel
There's nothing I wouldn't do for you
Just tell me what you want, what you need,
what you desire

I would steal for you, live, and die
I'll be your shelter, your protector, your guardian
The sun and moon and stars in your sky
Just to have you by my side is all I need
It breaks my heart knowing that it will never be

I want it so bad, I can taste it
But you don't – why?

The Hands of Time Move Forward

The fear of the unknown becomes me
The silence is screaming for the words I long to hear
The tortured heart and tormented soul
The pain is real as the tears overtake
what is left of my life

The waves of memories from yesterday's happiness
Have become the nightmares of tomorrow
I don't know how to go on living like this
I don't think I can with all of the sorrow

The fault is my own and no one else's
Inside the place where the pain dwells
The blame belongs to its rightful owner
I carry it through my living hell

The one thing I can not do is turn back the hands of time
Undo the pain that I've caused to myself
Waiting in the silence that I dread
Not knowing if it will ever be the way it once was

Please say that we can start over again
Don't let this be the end
I'm so sorry for this whole confusion
I miss our talks, I miss my friend

My Cries

The world that I thought was true
is now pushing me closer to the edge
I'm growing tired of holding on
and I feel like I'm losing my grip
Hanging by the words that once rang true
and are now proving false
Would you even care if I did go under
and if I did start to slip?

Was the truth just too much for you to take?
You can not find a place to hide behind the lies
Would you rather that I did not say anything at all?
Just go on pretending and not hearing my cries

You're always searching for the answer you want to hear
Won't listen to anything else or give anyone
a chance to understand
Putting a stop to everything you just shut everyone out
The emptiness is now the only thing that is so deep
and continues to surround

Given everything that we've shared
so openly and honestly
Not believing that the moment has already passed me by
If I had the opportunity I would do it all over again
The hope that there is still something left is the only
thing that keeps me alive

The Skies Grow Darker

The death beast has come to destroy
that which was once so strong and so true
I refuse to stop fighting and to just give up
and to lose hope of regaining the trust
The skies grow dark all around
as the fierce storm continues to rage within me
I am spinning out of control
as the waves are pounding against my shattered heart
The downpour on my soul is causing me
to lose my grip and sink further away
Lightening crashes violently as it lights up
the midnight sky in the world that I once knew
The uncharted terrains of the deep and unknown
have now become my battleground
Slipping through the cracks of the sheltered life
as the silence and fear paralyze me
The whirlwind blows and stirs up the heavy emotions
that I do not want to carry anymore
Emptiness has once again taken its toll
and has now become the only thing that I know
The guilt and sorrow cry out so loudly
but there is nothing here to comfort the lonely
I can no longer feel my body
as the memories overtake what is left of my life
The painful screams of hurt and torment
echo through the silence like rolling thunder
Exhaustion now takes over
and I can't stop the tears from falling from my eyes

My Heart and Soul Cry Out

The scars of my tortured being come to surface
as the fright tightens its grasp on my life
Changes have begun to take place
as it tries to reclaim the victory that once was mine
The words of yesterday still continue to haunt me
and there is no escape from them
My heart and soul cry out but the only answer to me
is bone-chilling silence
The insecurities are overwhelming me
as I regretfully re-live the mistakes that I've made
It's now beyond my control and I can't help
but wonder will there ever be an end to this?

The Masterpiece

Sometimes late at night I go down by the lake
to think about life for a while
I try to figure out why I do the things I do,
or better put, why I did the things I did
It was a beautiful masterpiece, a painting
of the best thing that's ever happened to me
I just ripped it apart
I remember my heart being much redder
and much brighter
I gaze at the stars and watch the light of the moon
dance upon the calmness of the water
It reminds me of how I used to be, so joyous
and happy and carefree
I take a deep breath of the brisk night air
that exists between you and me
The questions and concerns go through my mind
The gentle breeze that embraces me makes me feel
like I did not long ago, safe and protected,
the things that only can be provided
by a trustworthy friend
The rain starts to fall down from the heavens
like the tears that flow from my now empty heart

Separation

I don't know how much longer I can do this
Painting on this fake smile for the world to see
While deep inside I'm bleeding and dying
Living each and every day in complete misery

The confusion that once embraced me
So unbelievably tight in its grasp
Has now been replaced with absolute certainty
Don't say it's too late and that the time has passed

Wanting to understand why this can't be
Trying to carry on from day to day
Putting on a show like this doesn't bother me
Just pretending everything is going to be okay

But when no one is watching to judge me
That's when I feel like I can be myself
I give in to the depression and cry so uncontrollably
And hide behind the curtain
that separates me and the world

Suffering

You are always questioning,
never knowing how to get by
I just don't want to wonder anymore,
someone please tell me why
The one thing I'm sure of, the one thing that is not a lie
Is that the happiest day of my life
will be the day that I die

I sit here in this bone chilling emptiness,
while I try not to breathe
The haunting coldness grasps me so tight,
I just want to leave
All alone with my shattered soul,
wondering why I can not grieve
But I'm paralyzed by the silence,
so I wear a broken heart on my sleeve

Life is nothing but suffering,
time goes right out the window
The reasons why,
how come no one ever seems to know
Trying to stay strong,
trying to stay true but it's beyond my control
Why is it that the hardest part of holding on is letting go?

The Remains of My Broken Heart

Sitting in complete silence and waiting in total misery
for something to happen, but I don't know why
I know I shouldn't waste any more sweet time
waiting for you
It seems that I have also wasted all my tears crying
over you, someone who obviously doesn't care for me
I fell for a dream that has now been torn apart,
shattered into a million pieces like the remains of
my broken heart, which now lies bleeding helplessly
I have been trapped in this dark hole
and haven't seen the light of day for quite some time
You have humiliated me
and embarrassed me long enough
I fail to understand why you could do this to me
How you could do something like this to me
You shot me straight in the heart
You left me with no warning, no reason,
no explanation, no goodbye, no nothing...
just up and left, I'll never get over you walking away
You completely killed me
and left me with nothing but shattered dreams
I have never felt so empty inside, so alone, so dead
I've hit rock bottom
and it's a very cold and frightening place to be
The memories of a happy and comfortable yesterday
keep running through circles in my mind
Confusion has become a constant companion,
and I'm left completely lost in total isolation

You let me down so many times, walked all over me,
held me down and made me cry,
but I looked at you through the eyes of a fool
I didn't seem to care, I just kept coming back for more
we shared so much,
but I'm beginning to think that it wasn't true
Someone please tell me how a perfect love goes wrong
Was it ever real?
Did you ever really care for me?
I have wasted my tears, my secrets, my love, my life
I thought that time might help me win this game,
but it's slowly driving me insane
The thing I fear the most is that these wounds
will never heal, the pain that I feel is all too real
I just can't escape the ghost of you
Too much damage has been done
by your careless words,
too much which time cannot erase
Despite all the torture that you've put me through,
all of the pain and suffering and torment and misery,
I still love you
I know that I shouldn't
So help me God I still do and I always will
It's as if I am under kind of spell
and I will never be set free...

Shattered Dreams

Alas my love, I can finally say goodbye to you
Releasing the shattered dreams of a broken yesterday
Alas my love, the ghost of you will no longer haunt me
The time has come to be set free from these demons

There is a bright, exciting,
and fresh dawn on the horizon
The dark clouds have been lifted
from the depths of my soul
A new day is breaking,
an open invitation for new beginnings
Giving way to the healing warmth of the sun
which embraces my body

The doors which were once sealed shut
are slowly beginning to open
Stepping into the light that holds the key
for all opportunities for me
Now walking through the realms of all possibilities
that lay before me
I'm feeling as though I'm floating through the sky

Tranquility

I want to take a plunge into the calmness
of a sea of tranquility
I want to get lost in the blinding light
of those amazing eyes
I want to be part of the magic that can be found
in this amazing world
I want to hold you so tight
I want to dive into the warmth of your embrace
on a cold night
I want to run to you when I'm scared
of the obstacles life brings
I want to be able to hear your thoughts
and see your dreams
I want to be the blood that races through your veins
I want to be able to give you a pair of wings when
you want to fly
I want to be what completes your life
I want to be held tight in your arms
until the day that I die
I want to be the one to turn the golden key
and unlock your heart
I want to ease away your every pain
I want to feel your beautiful soul
I want to be part of the your endless dream

The Light of My Heart

I lie awake in my bed each night dreaming about you
I imagine how it would feel to hold you tight in my arms
Just to have your warm body close to mine
The only sound would be your heart beating next to mine
What I wouldn't give to get lost in your eyes

Tremble

You have touched me in a great way
I feel you in the depths of my soul
Your eyes are the stars in my heaven
They're always shining and so full of life
Your smile rescues me from harm
It's enough to make me tremble and shake
The sound of your voice is my saving grace
You have captured my heart from the beginning